Hide and Seek

Find the Wild Animal

By Cate Foley

Children's Press
A Division of Grolier Publishing
New York / London / Hong Kong / Sydney
Danbury, Connecticut

Photo Credits: Cover, p. 9, 10, 11, 13, 14, 15, 17, 18, 19, 21b, 21c, 21d © Indexstock; p. 5, 6, 7, 21a © Shane Moore/Animals Animals
Contributing Editor: Jennifer Ceaser
Book Design: MaryJane Wojciechowski

Library of Congress Cataloging-in-Publication Data

Foley, Cate.
  Find the wild animal / by Cate Foley.
    p. cm. — (Hide and seek)
  Includes bibliographical references and index.
  Summary: Challenges the reader to examine photographs and find the wild animals hiding in their surroundings, including monkeys, bears, and sloths.
  ISBN 0-516-23098-0 (lib. bdg.) — ISBN 0-516-23023-9 (pbk.)
  1.Mammals—Juvenile literature. 2. Camouflage (Biology)—Juvenile literature. [1. Camouflage (Biology) 2. Picture puzzles.] I. Title.

QL706.2.F66 2000
599.147′2—dc21   00-024580

Contents

1 Animals with Gray Fur   6

2 A Crocodile   10

3 An Animal with Spots   14

4 A Hyena   18

5 New Words   22

6 To Find Out More   23

7 Index   24

8 About the Author   24

Look closely.

Do you see the animals up
in the tree?

This is a mother sloth and her baby.

Their fur is as gray as the **bark**.

Look closely.

Do you see the animal napping near the water?

This is a crocodile.

Its **bumpy hide** blends in with the rock.

11

Look closely.

Do you see the animal sitting under the tree?

This animal with spots is a leopard.

It hides in the **shade** to surprise its **prey**.

15

Look closely.

Do you see the animal resting in the dirt?

This is a hyena.

Its fur is as brown as the ground.

Which wild animal do you like the best?

New Words

bark (bark) the covering of a tree

bumpy (bum-pee) having hard bumps

hide (hyd) the covering of an animal

prey (pray) animals that are hunted for food

shade (shayd) a place out of the sun

To Find Out More

Books
Animal Hide-And-Seek
by Teddy Slater and Donna Braginetz
Bantam Doubleday Dell Books For Young Readers

Wild Animals
by Brian Wildsmith
Oxford University Press

Web Sites
Animals Wild & Wonderful
http://www.jspca.org.za/antics/animal_main.html
This site has lots of interesting facts about different wild animals.

San Diego Wild Animal Park
http://www.sandiegozoo.org/wap/homepage.php3
Check out your favorite wild animals at this online zoo. There are pictures and information about the animals at the park.

Index

bark, 6
bumpy, 10

crocodile, 10

hide, 10
hyena, 18

leopard, 14

prey, 14

shade, 14
sloth, 6

About the Author
Cate Foley writes and edits books for children. She lives in New Jersey with her husband and son.

Reading Consultants
Kris Flynn, Coordinator, Small School District Literacy, The San Diego County Office of Education

Shelly Forys, Certified Reading Recovery Specialist, W.J. Zahnow Elementary School, Waterloo, IL

Peggy McNamara, Professor, Bank Street College of Education, Reading and Literacy Program